My State

MONTANA

By Christina Earley

TABLE OF CONTENTS

A Crabtree Seedlings Book

Crabtree Publishing
crabtreebooks.com

School-to-Home Support for Caregivers and Teachers

This book helps children grow by letting them practice reading. Here are a few guiding questions to help the reader build his or her comprehension skills. Possible answers appear in red.

Before Reading:

- What do I know about Montana?
    - *I know that Montana is a state.*
    - *I know that Montana has mountains.*

- What do I want to learn about Montana?
    - *I want to learn which famous people were born in Montana.*
    - *I want to learn what the state flag looks like.*

During Reading:

- What have I learned so far?
    - *I have learned that Helena is the state capital of Montana.*
    - *I have learned that there are more than 700 miles (1,127 km) of trails at Glacier National Park.*

- I wonder why...
    - *I wonder why the state flower is the bitterroot.*
    - *I wonder why there are so many deer, elk, and antelope in Montana.*

After Reading:

- What did I learn about Montana?
    - *I have learned that you can dig for sapphires at Gem Mountain.*
    - *I have learned that the state animal is the grizzly bear.*

- Read the book again and look for the glossary words.
    - *I see the word **capital** on page 6, and the word **legendary** on page 18. The other glossary words are found on pages 22 and 23.*

MONTANA
Hi! My name is Kinsley. Welcome to Montana!

I live in Missoula. I can see Mount Sentinel from my house!

Many people go fly-fishing for trout in Missoula.

Montana is in the northwestern United States. The **capital** is Helena.

Fun Fact: Billings is the largest city in Montana.

The state animal is the grizzly bear.

The bitterroot is the state flower.

We grow a lot of wheat in Montana. Some of it is used to make bread.

Fun Fact: Montana is one of the states that **produces** the most wheat in the U.S.

My state flag is blue. The state **seal** is in the middle.

There are many deer, elk, and antelope in Montana.

My family explores Glacier National Park. Sometimes we see mountain goats.

Fun Fact: There are more than 700 miles (1,127 km) of trails at Glacier National Park.

My family and I like to visit the **ghost town** of Bannack.

We dig for **sapphires** at Gem Mountain.

Animator Brad Bird was born in Montana. **Legendary** NBA coach Phil Jackson was also born in Montana.

Fun Fact: Jeannette Rankin, the first woman elected to the United States Congress, was born in Missoula, Montana.

I watch the snow geese and tundra swans at Freezeout Lake.

I enjoy skiing down the mountain at Big Sky.

Glossary

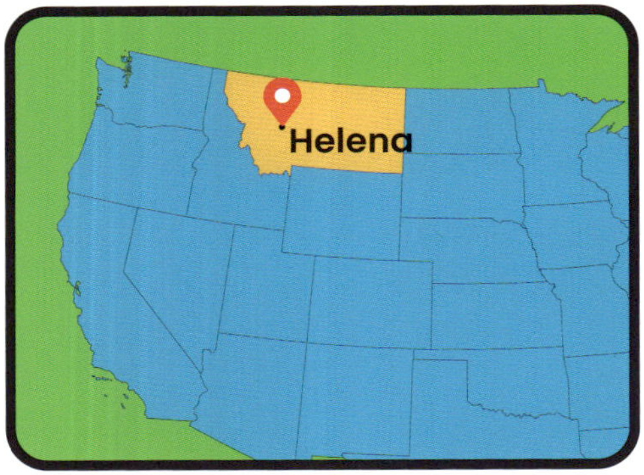

capital (cap-ih-tuhl): The city or town where the government of a country, state, or province is located

ghost town (goast toun): A town that no longer has any people living in it

legendary (lej-ihn-day-ree): Very famous

produces (pruh-doos-es): Makes or grows something for sale or use

sapphire (sa-fy-er): A precious stone that is usually blue

seal (seel): A special design that is used on important papers and other items

Index

About the Author

Christina Earley lives in sunny South Florida with her husband and son. She enjoys traveling around the United States and learning about different historical places. Her hobbies include hiking, yoga, and baking.

Written by: Christina Earley
Designed and Illustrated by: Bobbie Houser
Series Development: James Earley
Proofreader: Melissa Boyce
Educational Consultant: Marie Lemke M.Ed.

Photographs:
Alamy: Ingemar Magnusson: p. 17, 23; PA Images: p. 18 left
Shutterstock: kan_khampanya: cover; DosanJones: p. 3; Jon Bilous: p. 4; Cannon Colegrove: p. 5; Volina: p. 6, 22; Dennis W Donohue: p. 8; Frank L Junior: p. 9; Charles Lemar Brown: p. 10-11; Scorpp: p. 11, 23; railway fx: p. 12, 23; Tom Reichner: p. 13; TheBigMK: p. 14; Lyonstock: p. 14-15; Rob Crandall: p. 16, 22; Sam Aronov: p. 18 right, 22; Kruize Derek Christensen: p. 20; alexfe: p. 21
whitehouse.gov: p. 19

Crabtree Publishing

crabtreebooks.com 800-387-7650

Printed in the U.S.A./072023/CG20230214

Published in Canada
Crabtree Publishing
616 Welland Avenue
St. Catharines, Ontario
L2M 5V6

Published in the United States
Crabtree Publishing
347 Fifth Avenue
Suite 1402-145
New York, New York, 10016

Library and Archives Canada Cataloguing in Publication
Available at Library and Archives Canada

Library of Congress Cataloging-in-Publication Data
Available at the Library of Congress

Hardcover: 978-1-0398-0523-1
Paperback: 978-1-0398-0555-2
Ebook (pdf): 978-1-0398-0619-1
Epub: 978-1-0398-0587-3